# AN EYE ON HEAVEN

## The Biblical Bosses of Norwich Cathedral

### From the Creation to Solomon

Phillip McFadyen

First published in Great Britain 1999
Norwich Cathedral Publications Ltd
12 The Close
Norwich
NR1 4DH

ISBN 0 9535493 1 3

All profits from the sale of this booklet are covenanted to:
The Friends of Norwich Cathedral

Printed in Great Britain by
Catton Print, Norwich.

# Contents

# FOREWORD

Now that it is possible to study the bosses in the vault roof of the nave in the cathedral, not just by craning the neck or using the mirrors, but because of Julia Hedgecoe's remarkable photographs and Martial Rose's scholarly studies, the many, many people who visit are able to go further than marvelling at the expertise of those 15th century craftsmen who created them. Not only expertise but vision – vision which Phillip McFadyen in this book, appropriately called *An Eye on Heaven*, quite rightly sees that we in the late 20th century need to catch. For the 15th century craftsmen these Old Testament stories were *their* stories; they designed their figures in "modern dress" because what these familiar stories had to tell and teach was relevant to the troubled times in which they lived. So, too, for us. Phillip makes sense of them for us.

In times now as troubled as theirs, the stories in the early books of the Bible are stories which have as much relevance to our own century. We need to take to heart and put into practice what the stories these bosses present have to teach *us* – not easy but so necessary. Phillip McFadyen's presentation of them, in writing and illustrations, and his comment on each of the Old Testament bosses can do this for us.

Dorothy Bartholomew

# AN EYE ON HEAVEN
## The Biblical Bosses of Norwich Cathedral

## FROM THE CREATION TO SOLOMON

The early books of the Bible contains some of the finest stories ever told. Sadly, having survived 3000 years of telling, they are in danger of being forgotten. Why should this be in an age that claims to be the most literate since time began? The answer to this question might have something to do with the way we receive information.

Despite an explosion of information technology our vision is often limited to a television monitor. The 'box' is readily accessible in most of the rooms we occupy. In the 15th century, when many men and women could not write, they too received their information pictorially. If they visited Norwich Cathedral they would have received visual messages, not through a box but through a boss.

The bosses of Norwich Cathedral communicate visually some of the best loved Bible stories. A galaxy of them dazzle from the vaults of the Cathedral roof. These Nave bosses present the history of salvation from Genesis to Doomsday communicating their message in the media of their day.

Only fragments of the Norwich Mystery plays have survived, unlike those of York, Chester and Wakefield. However, the Cathedral bosses provide us with the best guide as to what they might have contained. They represent a frozen picture in stone of how the actors would have looked in a tableau. Each boss represents a scene as it might have appeared on a cart as it trundled through the streets. From such a vantage point, players would declaim their interpretation of the Bible story, making it live for the people who came to watch.

For centuries these stories in stone have been only dimly viewed even by the exceptionally long sighted. Now they have been captured by the telephoto lens and we can appreciate the skill and artistry involved in the creation of this amazing cycle. Norwich Cathedral contains the largest collection of story bosses in the world. They are a testimony to the interest and importance of the art of story telling in the late Middle Ages. We are indebted to Julia Hedgecoe for making these hidden treasures more accessible to us. The publication of her fine photographs together with the expertise of Martial Rose has revealed both the imagery and its meaning. The iconography that they have brought to light has helped me to use these story bosses for their original purpose of conveying Bible stories and their message to those seeking an answer to life's questions.

This little book concentrates on how the world began; at least as far as the Old Testament is concerned. Genesis tells us that God may be in his heaven but all is not well with his world. God's command to go forth and multiply is frustrated. From Creation to Solomon things go wrong repeatedly. Innocence is lost, women are not fruitful and all that multiplies is violence. After only seven chapters the earth is seen to be filled with wickedness. As confusion breaks out, the patriarchs, those nomadic shepherds, step out in faith seeking to live in concert with God's original plan. Fifteenth century people understood these themes very well. Having experienced a catalogue of catastrophes – ambitious landowners and ecclesiastical shepherds misbehaving, the economy crippled by the legacy of the Black Death, the Wars of the Roses, all this was seen to be presaged in the Genesis narrative.

These Old Testament stories, which made such sense to the people of the 15th century, are equally relevant to us today. The bosses look down on those trying to make sense of their lives. They are a testimony to those of any age who have the imagination to dress the patriarchs in the clothes of their own period and look heavenward for inspiration and guidance. When we are confronted with questions of life and death, these stories in stone provide an arena for reference. Having an 'eye on heaven' enables us to make some connections with our own situation. May these medieval carvings remind us of something we are in danger of losing.

*Phillip McFadyen*
*Ranworth*

# Finding the Bosses Described in this Book

All the bosses described are to be found in the first seven bays of the Nave in Norwich Cathedral going from east (over the choir) to west.

The centre boss is the largest and tells the main story in the bay. The surrounding bosses add to the story.

The book considers 26 bosses

Bay 1    Numbers 1–7

Bay 2    Numbers 8–10

Bay 3    Numbers 11–14

Bay 4    Numbers 15–20

Bay 5    Number 21

Bay 6    Numbers 22–23

Bay 7    Numbers 24–26

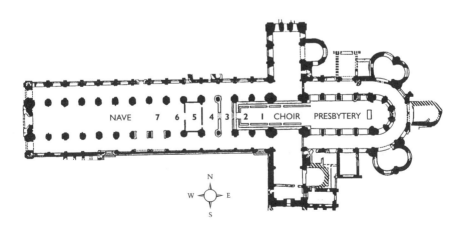

## *1. The Creation of Light*

A medieval player might stand in a darkened space holding
a blazing torch and wearing a golden mask. To his audience
he would be the sun, the source of life and light. For our
stories in stone to unfold there must be illumination and the
first boss in the East of the nave provides it. Here the
Genesis story begins with a dramatic symbol; but this light is
benign. It gently encourages our story to unfold. However,
this first boss has political as well as theological significance.
The sun symbol was strongly associated with the ruling
house of York. It was politically correct during the reign of
Edward IV to present light in terms of a Yorkist badge. It is
theologically correct to interpret this boss in terms of the
Genesis narrative: 'And God said, Let there be Light'(1.3).
It is a very dramatic moment in the Genesis text, since prior
to the creation of light the earth had been a formless place of
chaotic darkness. The watery chaos is held back by the
'wind' or 'spirit' of God moving over the silent waters of
confusion. The first word God utters is to call light into
being. This blazing boss symbolises the illumination that
God's word brings. Now we can see things clearly. The dark
is separated from the light. Day one comes into being. Time
and space have meaning. The scene is set for history to
unfold. 'And God saw the light was good' (1.4).
Benevolence is the sentiment expressed here. Shining, as it
does, in the east end of the nave it reflects the rays of the
rising sun. The story of salvation is set in motion by a stone
luminary suspended high above our heads. Whatever may
follow we are assured that 'the light shines in the darkness
and the darkness has not overcome it' (John.1.5).

## 2. God blesses his creation

Here we have a magnificent boss presenting us with a resplendent image of the 'old man in the sky' that modern theology is keen for us to forget. Yet the story-telling dramatists of the fifteenth century needed a strong awe-inspiring figure to represent the Creator God who called into being 'all things visible and invisible'. Fixed high above the nave, this magisterial figure in red and gold raises one hand in blessing while the other holds a pair of dividers with which to measure the sum of all things. He stands flanked by a lion and a unicorn which have come to represent regality and power. The king of beasts sits submissive while the mysterious unicorn kneels in homage. The fruitful world which God has called into being is represented by the lush foliage of green and gold, a perfect foil to the radiant red figure who beams down on us.

The first chapter of Genesis presents us with a powerful God who can control events with a word and who names his creations as they come into being. He is well pleased with his work and when it is completed on the sixth day, he blesses his creatures saying, 'Be fruitful and multiply, and fill the earth and subdue it and have dominion over the fish of the seas and over the birds of the air and over every living thing that moves upon the earth' (1.29).

The question for us is whether we have fulfilled this command as good stewards or have we been exploiters who rape and ravage creation for our own greedy ends? The Genesis story tells us of an ecological balance in which man has a position of great trust and responsibility. A benign ruler, who holds creation in check with a commission and a blessing, might well be disturbed by how we have responded to his divine challenge. Is there a hint of anxiety in the eyes of those beasts entrusted to our charge?

4

## 3. The angels of creation

Angels were very popular in medieval mythology and they appear constantly in ecclesiastical art of the period. They cover rood screens in their nine-fold orders and dominate hammer beam roof spaces. Here we find two in attendance on God blessing his creation. The angel in the north is dressed entirely in feathers, modelling a costume often employed by the players in the Mystery Cycle who performed this role. Feathered trousers were the fashion for angels and this angel is suitably attired for his northerly position. The angel of the south, which we see illustrated here, is more symmetrical, with half spread golden wings, he kneels in adoration, his hands upheld in praise.

In the creation story angels do not make personal appearances except to expel Adam and Eve from the garden after their act of disobedience (3.24). During the creation narrative there is only one player and that is God himself who is in full control of the events in chapter one. However, there is a sense in which God is not alone but engages in a dialogue with himself. e.g. 'Let there be Light' (1.3), 'Let the earth put forth vegetation' (1.11) and finally 'Let us make man in our image, after our likeness' (1.26). In the early chapters of Genesis angels represent the very presence of God. Their only function is to convey messages. The word 'angel' means literally 'messenger'. The supposed dialogue we overhear in the creation story suggests a kind of heavenly court discussing the world as it comes into being. We are not meant to think of God as some kind of divine committee, but there is a sense in which ideas formulate and develop within the Godhead, and the Christian doctrine of the Trinity is a development of this concept. Our medieval craftsman reminds us that besides being in attendance, angelic spirits have a mediating role of bringing God's presence into our perception. May they continue to remind us of God's overarching concern for his world and help us to praise him for the glories of his creation.

## 4. Creation of fish, fowl, and beasts

A cluster of bosses beautifully illustrates the rich variety of wildlife called into being by the creator God of Genesis.

'Let the waters bring forth swarms of living creatures and let birds fly above the earth across the firmament of the heavens'. (1.20)

'Let the earth bring forth living creatures according to their kinds, cattle and creeping things and beasts of the earth according to their kinds'. (1.24)

The medieval artists have delighted in representing a swirling shoal of fish suspended in the vaulting in a design that is both striking and strangely modern. The fowl are represented by an eagle and a white swan. The eagle is magnificent in red and gold, his feathers reminiscent of the angel of creation. He glowers down against a blue sky. In appearance he echoes that other great biblical eagle, the symbol of St. John's gospel, who is often seen proclaiming that 'in the beginning was the Word' (John 1.1). The word of God in Genesis allows creation to come into being rather than demanding an obedient response. 'Let the earth bring forth'. . . and so the swan sallies forth in gorgeous white plumage, decorated with golden spots and sporting a golden neckband. Like the white hart, she may have political significance. Both these creatures were associated with the rival house of Lancaster. For the Cathedral to survive the vagaries of the houses of Lancaster and York, it was wise for the Bishop to hedge his bets. It appears as if God is letting his creatures be, despite their political allegiances.

Perhaps there is a lesson here for our time. God's creation is rich in variety. It is possible for all his creatures to live together peaceably and to rejoice and value the differences that make up the richness of our world. If the 'sun' of York can shine on these Lancastrian creatures, then it is possible for those of opposing views to co-exist peaceably.

8

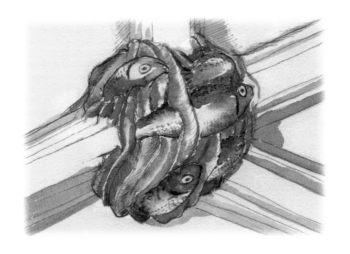

## 5. Creation of Adam and Eve

Two bosses showing God engaged in a 'hands on' method of creation. Both the man and the woman are very definitely God's handiwork. Adam is created by a master potter who forms him from 'the dust of the earth' (2.7). Eve is created by God adopting the role of a surgeon who puts the man to sleep (under anaesthetic almost) so that 'while he slept he took one of his ribs and closed up the place with flesh', the rib being used to create the woman.

Having moved into the second creation story found in Genesis chapter two, God is much more active and willing to adopt human characteristics. No longer is he the remote figure of chapter one who calls things into being simply by uttering the word. Here we have a different presentation. Now we see a God who is more involved. Not only does he model from clay the man and the woman himself, he also constructs beasts and birds by the same process, bringing them to the man to name (1.19). The reason for all this wildlife is simply that the man should not be lonely (1.18). However, fur and feathered friends are no substitute for human companionship and the woman is found to be the perfect partner, so that they eventually become 'one flesh' – one in mind and purpose.

The nakedness of the man is very natural in this boss. Nakedness has always been a problem in Christian art and the only way the nude figure might be legitimately portrayed is in the Adam and Eve story. The artist has achieved an unselfconscious presentation and we can rejoice in the ingenuousness of these figures who seem perfectly at ease in the presence of their maker. This is a God who is deeply involved with humankind and is concerned for our well-being. Have we lost something of the innocence portrayed here? Our sophisticated world can learn much from the childlike presentation found in these naive bosses.

## 6. The Fall

This splendid boss holds the central place in the first bay of the nave.
Adam and Eve stand below a leafy tree burgeoning with golden apples.
In the centre of this profusion coils a very feminine looking serpent which
offers tasty fruit to the naked pair, both of whom have their hands full of
the ripe produce. This is a full-blooded fall, no hesitancy here. Both
Adam and Eve appear to be enjoying munching the forbidden fruit.
They are willingly led on by their serpent mentor who holds sway in the
tree. The whole boss is beautifully carved, making full use of the three
dimensional effect. One surprising detail is that the tree is sprouting, not
from the good soil of Eden, but out of a pot! The reason for this
horticultural feature is that the boss is again reflecting the mystery play
model. The cart that transported this tableau would have needed a pot to
contain the tree of knowledge – its central prop.

The story known as 'The Fall' is a tale of wilful disobedience. The man
and the woman have complete liberty to enjoy the delights of the paradise
garden. There is only one condition, they must not eat of the tree of
Knowledge. To do so is to become like God. To become like God is to
disturb the balance God had created. Snatching at equality with God
results in a disturbance in the equilibrium. The man and the woman
discover their nakedness and hide. God, who has been their friend, is
now seen as an enemy to avoid. The relationship is broken, and
humankind begins the long quest or search for fulfilment. Medieval
theology understood this to be resolved in the birth of Christ who is seen
as the second Adam. Christ is the obedient son, who empties himself
rather than usurp God's authority (Phil.2.5–11). Instead of covering up
his vulnerability, he is naked, exposed on a tree of which he is the fruit of
redemption. This boss exactly parallels the first bay of bosses showing the
New Testament story and is seen as a 'type', or prophetic image, of the
birth of Christ. The old Adam prefigures the new.

# 7. The story of Cain

Two bosses concentrate on the figure of Cain to the exclusion of his younger brother Abel. One shows the elder brother as a fugitive after the killing of his younger brother. Cain, the tiller of the soil, runs across the roof, fleeing from his cursed state. 'When you till the ground, it shall no longer yield to you its strength; you shall be a fugitive and a wanderer on the earth' (Gen.4.12).

The other boss which we see here depicts the killing of Cain and is in direct contradiction with Scripture where Cain cries out 'Whoever finds me will slay me' (4.15). The Lord replies, 'Not so! if anyone slays Cain, vengeance shall he taken on him sevenfold'. The boss that relates the killing of Cain is based on an apocryphal story about Lamech, a blind archer who, wanting to keep in training, invites a young lad to direct his aim at a moving quarry. The lad discerns some movement in the bushes and guides Lamech's bow to the spot. Unfortunately, the quarry proves to be the hapless Cain who is shot through the heart. The disconsolate Lamech (dressed in the clothes of God) looks on with the unfortunate boy who, according to the legend, is beaten to death by Lamech, the recipient of the sevenfold curse of Gen. 4.15. This sad tale displays the medieval fascination with the moody elder son of Adam. In common with many tales from the Old Testament it seems as if God favours the younger over the older son. Jacob is blessed instead of Esau, Joseph rises over his brothers, David is chosen in preference to his seven older brothers. The message is that God does not judge by outward appearance, he looks into the heart of a man. Cain was angry when his brother found favour and was warned that his anger was like a demon 'crouching at the door'. He was encouraged to master it. Sadly, according to the tale, it mastered him and he killed his brother. The image of the fugitive is one that haunts us still. Those who drive themselves out of human society are never beyond God's help. According to the Genesis story, Cain receives the Lord's protection (4.15) but there always remains the possibility of mishap, as this story in stone vividly relates.

## 8. The Great Flood

The story of the flood is common to the ancient people of the 'fertile crescent' of Mesopotamia, and the Genesis version contains many of the characteristics found in the Babylonian 'myth of Gilgamish'. Possibly the folk tales of primitive peoples retained a memory of a total devastation which wiped out the known civilisation such as it was. Certainly, water was not only a source of life but also a cause of death. Flash flooding in the desert region of Judea causes more deaths today than heat-stroke. What is important for us is the interpretation that the Bible gives this story. Our boss sets the scene very well. Noah is busy constructing the ark in accordance with God's detailed instructions (Gen.6.14–16). He looks contented in his work, as a medieval craftsman might well be. The Noah of Genesis may have looked like this having 'found favour in the eyes of the Lord . . . a righteous man, blameless in his generation; Noah walked with God' (Gen.6.8–9). His family reap the benefits of this right relationship and they too are invited into the ark. A number of bosses show the family carrying some of the creatures to be saved. A white spotted ewe and a golden ram are brought by one of Noah's sons while his daughter-in-law cunningly conveys a hat full of birds safely through the rising waters. The Flood is seen as a direct consequence of a rising tide of wickedness and violence (Gen.6.11). God is determined to make a fresh start with a clean sweep. Had not Noah found favour all might have been lost according to the Genesis account. In the gospels we have a picture of Jesus weeping a flood of tears over the wickedness and violence of Jerusalem (Luke 19.41–44). Such tears will cleanse a world of the need for retribution. This is a cautionary tale and maybe our world needs reminding that violence and hate can only lead to destruction. Better it is to walk with God, content in the knowledge that he has a plan he can fulfil, if we will only co-operate.

## 9. The Ark sets sail

Once the preparations are made, Noah, his family and the animals are safely stowed on board the ark. The flood waters rise as 'two fountains of the great deep burst forth and the windows of heaven are opened' (Gen.7.11). As the waters increase, the ark 'rises high above the earth'. Our boss, high above the nave, shows us Noah, his wife and their anxious passengers looking out as the rain falls on the earth 'forty days and forty nights'. So that 'every living thing is blotted out from the face of the earth' (Gen.7.23).

As the waters subside the ark comes to rest on the mountains of Ararat. Noah opens his window and sends forth a raven. One of the Norwich bosses displays the errant raven, who is brown rather than black, gorging on the drowned remains of what looks like a pantomime horse with brown spots. Noah then sends forth a dove, but the dove finds no place to settle and returns. Seven days later she is sent again, this time returning with a freshly plucked olive branch (Gen.8.11) – a sign that the waters had subsided. Sent on a third mission, the dove fails to return. So Noah disembarks to re-populate the earth under the sign of a rainbow, a symbol of a new covenant between God and man. The earth is again at peace. The positioning of these bosses indicates the medieval conviction that the story of the flood was to be understood as a type prefiguring the New Testament account of the Baptism of Christ. Certainly we can see the connection. Water is common to both stories, so is the covenant idea in which an agreement is ratified between God and his people. Baptism is a sign of our entry into the new community of Christ. It symbolises our dying and rising with him. Originally, baptism was by total immersion. The candidate was nearly drowned then hauled up gasping for breath. This is a powerful symbol, which demonstrates that the newly baptised Christian is leaving an old sinful life and entering a new creation. The story of Noah is a tale which illustrates new beginnings. Forgiveness and a fresh start are promised and the olive branch reminds us we are called to live at peace with God and our fellow creatures.

## 10. Noah plants a vine

The medieval artist often had a strong sense of humour and many of the mystery plays contain parts for ribald characters. The shepherds are often comic figures, rustic and raucous. Here, high above the nave, we have two bosses meant to make us smile if not blush.

The subject matter is the little known story from Gen.9.20–29 in which Noah discovers the delights and dangers of the grape. In this boss we see him planting the fruiting vine in the earth with the help of a dibble. He is almost enveloped by the fruit and foliage. In another boss Noah is exposed as a figure of fun. The boss shows two of his sons, finding him drunk on his newly discovered produce, as he displays his nakedness to the full view of the nave below.

This is not strictly in accordance with the Genesis version. True, Noah does get drunk and is found 'uncovered' by Ham who tells his brothers Shem and Japheth. They discreetly enter the tent backwards in an attempt to throw a cloak over their father without looking at him (9.23). When Noah recovers he rewards Shem and Japheth for trying to protect his modesty, whereas Ham receives a cursing! The medieval players often had fun with this theme of drunkenness, perhaps it was as much of a problem then as it is now. The Chester Mystery Cycle portrays Mrs. Noah drunk on entering the ark. The Norwich bosses have Noah being uncovered rather than protected by his sons. This is a far cry from the innocence of the Eden Garden when nakedness was not a problem and the vine with its delights and dangers was not discovered.

21

## 11. The tower of Babel

The story of the tower of Babel is an attempt by ancient writers to explain our polyglot status. A world with a diversity of tongues needs some understanding. How is it that we have so many languages when everyone knows that English in its seventeenth century version is the one spoken in heaven! Seriously, since time began communication has been impeded by people not understanding each other. This does require some form of explanation.

The Babel story from which we get our 'babble,' reminds us that in God's original plan not only were human beings meant to live together in innocency and peace, we were also meant to communicate with God and each other. In the Genesis story so far we have lost our innocence; peace has been disrupted, now communications are about to falter. Why? Gen.ll.l-9 tells us of humankind's overarching ambition, the same besetting sin we learnt of in the garden of Eden. Men migrate, find a level space and plan to make 'themselves a name' by 'building a city and a tower with its top in the heavens'.

The Ziggurats of Mesopotamia are the models for this story, but medieval masons had a fifteenth-century fortified city gateway in mind. Here is another example of the artist firmly placing the Bible story in his own culture and context. The medieval city state was a fortified walled enclosure with a tightly organised system of goverment. Those who built them shared similar ambitions to those in the Genesis story. Anyone absorbed in empire building is in danger of losing contact with reality, if not causing confusion and mayhem. The stonemason at work on our boss looks totally immersed in his task. He is surrounded by the tools of his trade. All of these were used daily in the construction of this Cathedral – erected, we hope, not that man might 'make a name for himself' but rather that God's name might be glorified in a place where men and women from many nations might communicate with him.

## 12. Abraham entertains

The story of Abraham marks a new beginning in the Genesis story. The first eleven chapters have related a series of disasters – the fall, the flood and the Babel incident. Now we find a righteous man who is willing to take risks for God rather than grab what he can get. He is obedient even when the odds are stacked against him. Setting off on a journey 'not knowing where he was to go' as the writer of the book of Hebrews comments, Abraham is the great example of a faith surviving a number of tests. On his journeying we find him entertaining angels unawares. The story of Abraham's hospitality is set by the oaks of Mamre (Gen.18). Abraham is the archetypal nomad and, like the Bedouin traveller today, he lives in a tent accompanied by sheep and goats and other members of his tribe. Unfortunately, Abraham has no children by his wife Sarah. This is seen as a great disgrace especially as God has promised Abraham he will be 'the father of a great nation' (12.2) and that Sarah 'shall be the mother of nations' (17.16). As they are both well on in years (ninety nine and ninety respectively) this must be difficult to believe and Abraham can be forgiven for a surreptitious snigger (17.17). Not long after this Abraham has three visitors, and in accordance with eastern hospitality offers them 'a little water and a morsel of bread'. On their agreeing to stay for a while, Abraham has Sarah prepare a full scale banquet of cakes and fatted calf which is duly set before the mysterious visitors. Here we see one of them enjoying what appears to be a TV supper. The individual table is well furnished with food. The angels enquire after Sarah who, as is customary even today, is kept out of sight. Another boss in this bay shows her, not standing by a vent in the tent, but rather to the left of what looks like a sentry box but is in reality an arched doorway to a gabled fifteenth century building. She is not a Bedouin woman in purdah but a well dressed medieval lady. The good news is that she will conceive a child who will bring God's prophecy into being. Sarah like Abraham laughs at the idea. Their nervous laughter is commemorated in the name of their son Isaac which means 'God smiles'.

## 13. The sacrifice of Isaac

The story of Abraham being tested by God is one that is difficult for us to understand today. What sort of capricious God is it who can promise Abraham he will father a great nation then require him to offer his son as a human sacrifice?

Medieval people had no such qualms. The subject was popular and receives more than one treatment on the nave roof. Some sixty years earlier the subject was used for the famous Florentine competition between Brunelleschi and Ghiberti for the great commission to cast the famous 'gates of paradise' Baptistery doors. Our medieval artists may not have the same degree of Renaissance finesse but they give a vigorous vernacular treatment to this difficult subject.

In the boss which depicts this scene, the young child kneels on the medieval altar. Abraham in a stylish upturned hat wields a large sword but looks away in distress at what he is required to do. The designers of this boss saw it foreshadowing the sacrifice of Christ on Calvary. The sacrifice of the mass recalls the offering of God's son as an act of selfless obedience and faith. Abraham is tested by God almost beyond the limits of human endurance. Fortunately this sacrificial slaying of human life and hope is averted. An angel intervenes and a 'ram caught in a thicket' is provided (Gen. 22.13) As Abraham has survived the test by not withholding his only son, God swears to multiply his descendants 'as the stars of heaven' (22.17). In another boss we see how this promise is brought into being. A wife is found for Isaac from among Abraham's own people. Chapter twenty-four of Genesis describes how Abraham's servant seeks out a wife for Isaac. This romantic story has all the ingredients of a tale from Sheherazade's 'Arabian Nights'. Rebekah's kindness in providing water for the camels results in a marriage proposal. This is not just an arranged marriage, Rebekah is given a choice. She is willing to go to meet Isaac and as the story is told, it is very obviously a love match (24.62–67).

## 14. Esau and Jacob

God's promise to Abraham suffers a number of setbacks in the story of these two brothers. Not everything is as straightforward as we might expect. Firstly Rebekah, like her mother-in-law Sarah before her, has difficulty in conceiving children. When she does, twins are found to be struggling within her womb (Gen.25.22). This is an ominous sign, for the brothers do not get on together and neither will their descendants. The story is another example of the fact that God is free to choose how his promise will be fulfilled. As with Adam's sons it is the younger who will be preferred over the older.

The boys are very different. Twins they may be, but identical they certainly are not. At birth Esau is red and hairy, while Jacob is smooth and grasping. When they grow up Esau prefers the outdoor life of hunting while Jacob stays quietly in the tent cooking. The boss of Esau well portrays his outgoing nature. In a soldier's uniform he carries a bow and a trophy from the hunt. Jacob is very obviously his mother's favourite and she is determined to see him prosper. She busily prepares a deception so that Jacob may gain the birthright and blessing that should have go to his elder brother. When Esau is in the field she elaborately disguises Jacob to resemble his hairy brother. The boss which deals with this subject shows the blind Isaac lying in bed as Esau sets off for the hunt. On his left is Jacob well disguised, kneeling to receive his father's blessing by deception.

We might wonder at the elaborate lengths to which Jacob and his mother go to deceive the ageing Isaac, so that Esau, is denied his father's blessing. This is a cautionary tale which reminds us that even in a patriarchal society nothing must he taken for granted. God can overturn our time-honoured institutions. He can make good use of the most unlikely material. Jacob not Esau is the one through whom the line of blessing will continue.

## *15. Jacob journeying*

The story of Abraham, Isaac and Jacob is the story of a nomadic people. God has promised them that they will father a great nation. He now promises them a land in which they will dwell (Gen.28.4). Before this can happen it is important that Jacob be schooled and disciplined. Here we see him journeying to Paddan-aram, to the house of Laban his uncle, where his father Isaac had found Rebekah. It is important that the patriarchs make matches with their own people, not with the rather degenerate Canaanites who have been cursed since the time of Noah's indiscretions! The disappointed Esau sees no need for such precaution and looks to the tribe of Ishmael for his women.

Jacob leaves under a cloud. Obviously his brother is not pleased with him (Gen.27.41). In fact we see the beginnings of a blood feud. Rebekah comes to the rescue despatching Jacob to her brother's house in the hope that the fickle Esau will one day forget his grievance. She is also weary of the local girls and probably prefers to see her son wedded to one of her own family.

The mother-son relationship is well explored in these chapters of Genesis. Rebekah is determined to champion Jacob who shares her interests. Although Isaac obviously favours Esau he knows once his blessing has been conferred that there is no turning back. Jacob must leave and make his own way in life, portrayed here as a medieval pilgrim. The home loving Jacob must learn to step out on life's great adventure if he is to be used in God's purposes.

## 16. Jacob's dream at Bethel

On his way to Paddan-aram, Jacob stops overnight, taking a stone for a pillow. In the upper boss we see the wanderer sleeping on his back, his head on a red cushion rather than the stone. His staff lies beside him. Carved during the century that follows the publication of Chaucer's 'Canterbury Tales', Jacob is presented in the guise of the medieval pilgrim journeying from place to place as did the well travelled Margery Kempe from nearby Lynn in the fourteenth century. Medieval pilgrims would not have travelled alone as Jacob does here but they would be ready to perceive God's presence in a sacred place. Jacob, the forerunner of the medieval pilgrim, dreams of a ladder set up on the earth reaching into heaven. On it ascend and descend the angels of God. The lower boss shows this dream. Two winged angels climb the ladder which represents a bridge between heaven and earth, the sacred and the secular. The presence of God's messengers confirms that the door is open; God and man can communicate. Jacob hears the promise confirmed as he is about to be used for God's purposes in founding a people of God (Gen.28.13–15).

The New Testament picks up this idea of an open heaven. At the beginning of John's gospel, Jesus promises his disciples that they too will share Jacob's vision, for Jesus is the door and the gateway to God. Jacob celebrates the meaning of his dream by pouring oil on the stone on which he dreamed of the gate of heaven.

'Surely the Lord is in this place, and I did not know it. And Jacob was afraid and said: How awesome is this place! This is none other than the house of God, and this is the gate of heaven' (Gen.28.16–17).

In naming the site 'Bethel' Jacob is saying this is God's house. The same sentiment was shared by the medieval masons when they carved these bosses for the cathedral.

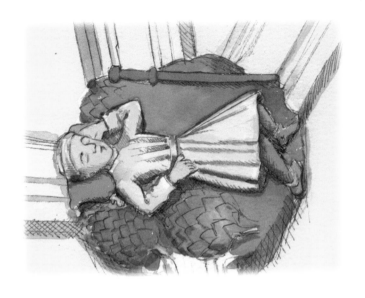

## 17. Jacob and his wives

Not only does Jacob retrace the journey his father's servant made, he finds himself at the same well. This time there is no need for an intermediary. Jacob acts on his own behalf, even removing the stone from the well so that the flocks can be watered. In Genesis 29 Rachel arrives as the keeper of her father's sheep. Jacob loses no time in kissing her and weeping over his find. After he introduces himself as her cousin, she runs off to report to her father Laban.

There is much kissing and embracing in the text as these nomads greet each other. Jacob agrees to tend Laban's sheep in exchange for his daughter's hand. After a seven year contract Jacob is married not to Rachel as he expected but to Leah, the older daughter. Jacob, the arch-deceiver, is being fed his own medicine. Laban cannot risk having a younger daughter married first, especially if she lacks her sister's beauty. Jacob has to agree to work another seven years for Rachel. Once this is agreed Jacob can marry Rachel within a week of his wedding to Leah! Here we see a medieval tonsured priest presiding over the ceremony.

Although this is a love match the pattern we noted earlier recurs. Rachel is the childless wife and the hated Leah gives birth to six sons and a daughter causing considerable enmity between the sisters, and an argument between Jacob and Rachel.

After liaisons with two maids Jacob eventually fathers two sons by Rachel, Joseph and Benjamin. The intrigue of these chapters may cause us to wonder at the ethics of the patriarchs. No such questions troubled the minds of our medieval forebears who simply place these stories in the domestic settings of their day. We too may find a number of parallels with the rich and famous of our day. Through the mess of human relationships God's purposes of forgiveness can still be traced, by those who look for it.

## *18. Jacob's sheep and goats*

Relations between Jacob and his father-in-law become somewhat strained, but Laban is reluctant to let his farm manager go. Jacob agrees to stay, on condition that they divide the flock. Jacob is to take the speckled goats and the spotted sheep. Laban confirms the plan but tries to trick Jacob again by removing the marked sheep before Jacob is able to take what is his. Jacob's cunning outstrips that of his father-in-law and he embarks on a complicated plan which involves peeling rods of poplar, almond and plane (Gen.30.31–41).

Here we see Jacob at work besides the stream, sporting an upturned hat, with sheep and goats around him. The plan to breed a stronger flock of sheep and a herd of goats is successful and Jacob grows rich with large flocks, servants and camels in abundance. This is cause for jealousy between Laban and Jacob as the text has it, 'Jacob saw that Laban did not regard him with favour as before' (Gen.31.2). Jacob and his family resolve to depart when Laban is occupied with sheep shearing. When Laban discovers what has happened he sets off in hot pursuit. Sadly there had been mistrust and grievance for twenty years, during which Jacob had complained that Laban has changed his wages some ten times. Now there is a resolution of the conflict and another boss shows Laban and Jacob shaking hands, with a close cropped son in attendance.

This boss of sheep feeding is a witness to a fifteenth century pastoral society which still had much in common with the stories of Genesis. Norfolk's economy was based on sheep rearing, the wool being exported to Flanders to make expensive cloth. Many of the fine churches of the region were financed by the wool trade and this Cathedral is the finest testimony to this wealth. The people who commissioned the bosses were fully aware of the disputes and deals of a sheep-farming community, as would be many of the masons. The stories of Jacob and his sheep would be very familiar to them and to the people who visited the cathedral. No doubt the oppressed medieval woman would have chuckled at the way Rachel manages to trick her father and get away with it!

## 19. Jacob wrestles with an angel

Having been reconciled to Laban, Jacob has to face his estranged brother
Esau from whom he cheated a birthright and a blessing. Instead of trying
to avoid Esau he seeks him out. Perhaps he feels more confident having
resolved his disputes with Laban and having flocks and herds of his own.
It is important that brothers learn to live together especially if they find
themselves in neighbouring farms. Jacob learns that Esau is coming to
meet him with some four hundred men. Fully expecting trouble, he
constructs a plan. He divides his company into two groups hoping that if
one is destroyed the others might escape. He also resorts to prayer
(Gen.32.9–12) and presents (32.13–21).

The prayer for deliverance is answered in the form of a struggle. When
Jacob is left alone, an angel wrestles with him all night until the break of
day. As the angel is unable to prevail over Jacob he puts Jacob's thigh out
of joint. Jacob will still not leave off the struggle until the angel blesses
him, renaming him Israel (meaning 'to strive with God'). The boss
presents the story in a restrained way. Jacob looks away from his
protagonist, fearful perhaps to look on God's messenger. The text tells us
that Jacob names the place Peniel (that is 'the face of God') saying, 'I
have seen God face to face and yet my life is preserved' (Gen.32.30).

The struggle with God continues as men and women wrestle with his
purposes. Jacob learnt to put his trust in God and not just in his own
machinations. The twister has become the one who prevails. In changing
his name from Jacob to Israel, he is changing his nature, but at some cost.
Jacob will limp. This struggle will leave its mark.

## 20. Jacob and Esau embrace

After the spiritual struggles of his dark night of the soul, Jacob has to lift up his eyes and face whatever the day may bring. He sees Esau coming with four hundred men (Gen.33.1). Although Jacob has committed himself to God by his prayers he is not above taking more practical precautions as well. The day before he had plied his brother with presents, putting a suitable distance between each gift to make the offerings seem larger. Now he looks to the safety of his immediate family, dividing them into groups, those closest to him in affection at the rear.

Having done all he can by way of prayer, presents and precautions he now prostrates himself seven times before his aggrieved brother as he approaches. What happens next is well described in the boss. Esau runs to greet his brother, falls on his neck and kisses him. The two brothers, so different in appearance and outlook, are reconciled. The scene that follows is full of oriental charm. Esau is introduced to Jacob's family who pay their respects. Esau tries to return Jacob's gifts but Jacob insists on him accepting, saying 'for truly to see your face is like seeing the face of God, with such favour have you received me. Accept, I pray you, my gift that is brought to you, because God has dealt graciously with me' (33.10–11).

So with some generosity and grace the brothers are reconciled. The story of struggle and animosity ends on a hopeful note. Something of the trust and innocence which was lost by self seeking in the garden of Eden is regained in the experience of trust and reconciliation.

## 21. Joseph in Egypt

The theme of journeying continues to occupy the writers of the book of
Genesis. As we journey down the nave of Norwich Cathedral we see the
story of Joseph set out in stone. This favourite son of Jacob rose to great
prominence in Egypt but not before he suffered at the hands of his
brothers. The story of his 'coat of many colours' is well known. His
brothers hated it as it was a badge of their father's favour. They were
determined to do away with this dreamer who fancied himself as one who
would have 'dominion over them'. Their opportunity arose when he came
to visit them as they pastured Jacob's sheep. The boss shows Joseph being
stripped of his precious coat prior to his being thrown into the pit
(Gen.43.23–24). The medieval craftsmen saw this as a 'type' of Christ's
humiliation and suffering, prefiguring the stripping and taunting Jesus
received at his Passion.

The story of Joseph takes a dramatic turn, when having been sold into
slavery, he becomes upwardly mobile. A rising visionary in Pharaoh's
Court he reorganises the country's economy with the aid of a seven year
plan. His far-sightedness, the cause of the dispute with his brothers,
becomes the means of his success in Egypt. What was for Joseph a
seeming disaster has been turned into an opportunity for growth. The
years of plenty were followed by years of famine, but Joseph's
management of Pharaoh's economy meant that there was grain enough
and to spare in Egypt. The brothers make several journeys to buy relief
from the famine. Not knowing of Joseph's successful career, they are
duped by him into total dependence on his largesse. Here we have a story
of reversed fortunes. There is a touching scene in Genesis 45 when
Joseph reveals himself to his frightened brothers. They may have stripped
him of his dream coat but he is prepared to be merciful and generous to
them now that they are, in fulfilment of his dream, under his jurisdiction.
Joseph interprets these events as a fulfilment of God's plan. God sent him
to Egypt to help his brothers (50.15–21). Again we have a story of
reconciliation and forgiveness that has much to say to us today.

## 22. Moses removes his boots

Joseph may have rescued his brothers by giving them the land of Goshen as a refuge, but the Egyptian people soon found that these visitors were getting too numerous. In Exodus chapter one we read that there arose in Egypt a King who did not know Joseph and enslaved his descendants to make bricks without straw (1.54). Pharaoh's attempts to cull the Israelites did not succeed in the case of Moses who was hidden from danger by his shrewd sister Miriam. The medieval craftsmen show her carefully entrusting him to the bulrushes, tightly swaddled as was their custom.

Discarded in the bulrushes by Pharaoh's daughter, Moses is brought up at the Egyptian court. As he grows up, Moses longs to help his suffering people. His first attempt to be their champion results in disaster and he finds himself fleeing to Midian in the Sinai peninsular. Like his forefathers, Moses meets the woman he is to marry at the local well. One of the bosses depicts another meeting place which was to leave a deep impression on Moses and change the course of religious history. In this boss we see Moses removing his boots for the place on which he stands is holy ground (3.5). The chapter tells us how Moses was minding sheep near the Mount of God. Somewhat dispirited by recent events he appears melancholic and depressed. Why else would he name his son 'Gersham' which means 'I have been a sojourner in a foreign land'? (2.21).

Depressed he may be and yet God can speak to him through a bush that appears to be burning. All that is required is that Moses attends to this sight. The practice of religion requires that we 'attend to' that which speaks of God. Through this experience we learn that in fact every bush is burning and the God of Moses reveals himself as one who is concerned about injustice and oppression. All that is required of us is a recognition that we stand in his presence. In removing his boots, Moses signals he is aware of the divine presence and is therefore more receptive to God's disclosures. God has much to reveal to those who will turn aside and investigate. These bosses repay our close attention, they blaze from above a message about holy ground.

## 23. *Pharaoh drowns in the Red Sea*

Moses was commissioned to tell Pharaoh to 'let my people go'. The story of the negotiations, with the accompanying ten plagues, is a cross between an oriental tale and long-drawn-out modern diplomacy. Middle Eastern politics remain incredibly protracted and are still largely about loss of face. Moses is immovable. He constantly repeats the message 'Let my people go' that they may serve God in the wilderness. Pharaoh's reluctance is understandable. Many ancient civilisations depended on the ready availability of slave labour. According to Exodus, the cities of Pitham and Ramases were built by the Hebrews and in any case, runaway slaves posed an economic threat. Like many politicians, Pharaoh plays for time until the Passover events plunge the nation into grief and mourning and the people are glad to see the children of Israel go, showering them with parting gifts of jewellery (12.35–37). There is a last minute hitch: Pharoah's changes his mind and resolves to give chase as the children of Israel cross the Red Sea. However, it is not only Pharaoh's heart which is hardened. The people themselves prove to be just as vacillating and fickle. At the sight of Pharoah's hosts they turn on Moses complaining that he has 'led them out to die in the wilderness' (14.11) . Moses takes command of the situation. A strong east wind blows all that night turning the sea into dry land and the people are able to cross in safely. The pursuing Egyptians were discomfited by the returning sea which covered the chariots and the horsemen', so that Israel saw 'the Egyptians dead upon the sea shore (14.30)'

In this boss we see Pharaoh himself, floating in full fifteenth-century armour alongside an upturned Yarmouth farm cart. He and some bobbing heads represent the 'great work which the Lord did upon the Egyptians'. Perhaps the medieval masons were reminding their own rulers of the fate that awaits those who would enslave God's pilgrim people. Whatever the hidden agenda, this is one of the most easily identified bosses and reminds those who walk beneath in the nave of that famous deliverance which gave Israel its identity as God's people.

## 24. Samson (Judges 13–16)

The title 'Judge' seems rather elevated for this champion prize fighter who takes a fancy for foreign women. The Judges of ancient Israel were charismatic leaders who took charge of the tribal battles that developed as Israel infiltrated the promised land. Like Wild West characters, they appear to have got into a number of scrapes and Samson is no exception. Apart from the fact he was forbidden strong drink as a Nazarite, (13.4–5) he might qualify as something of a modern day 'lad'. His preference for Philistine girls precipitates a number of arguments with the Philistines who occupied the coastal strip and were far more 'civilised' than the Israelites at this time. When he finds his new wife has cheated him, he smites them 'hip and thigh' with a great slaughter. On another occasion he brags that 'with a jawbone of an ass, heaps upon heaps, with the jaw of an ass I have slain a thousand men' (15.16). In this boss we see the mighty Samson carrying away the gates of the city of Gaza. One tucked under his arm and the other on his shoulder. He seems to be reminding the men of that city that if he wants to spend the night with a harlot, then it is none of their business (16.1–15). Certainly they should think again if they want to creep up on him. Sadly for Samson the men of Gaza would be avenged for this. Delilah is his next infatuation. She is more skilled then her predecessors and able to entice Samson, tantalising him to tell her wherein his great strength lies. Fond of riddles and pranks he plays a game of cat and mouse with his temptress until she pouts that he is mocking her with lies. How can he love her, she complains, if he will not share his secret? And so it was that 'she pressed him daily with her words so that his soul was vexed to death' (16.16, 17). Poor Samson confesses that his strength lies in his golden locks. While he sleeps on her lap, the hair is snipped and his strength sapped from him. Samson is taken captive, blinded, and made to grind corn. Eyeless in Gaza, the doomed champion has to wait for his hair to grow again before he is able to bring the house down on a Philistine party 'so that the dead he slew in his death were more than they which he slew in his life' (16. 30). Strong in his arm but rather weak in the head, Samson is still used for God's purposes, reminding the Philistines not to trifle with the Judges of Israel.

## 25. David and Goliath

If Samson can win by size, David can overcome by stealth. There comes
a time when the people of Israel clamour for a king 'like that of the other
nations'. There is some resistance to that idea. After all The Lord God
is their King. Eventually God agrees to this request and his prophet
Samuel anoints Saul as the first king of Israel. Sadly this experiment soon
goes astray. Saul becomes moody and difficult. Part of the reason for this
was the incident we see represented in this boss.

Again the Philistines are being troublesome. This time they have elected
a champion, one Goliath of Gath to fight again an Israelite challenger.
Goliath is massive and Saul and all Israel are 'dismayed'. However, the
'ruddy' young shepherd David, from Bethlehem, decides to take on this
Philistine giant, while visiting his brothers at the front. He persuades
Saul that the Lord that delivered David 'from the paw of a lion and a
bear' while he was minding sheep will deliver him from the hand of this
Philistine. Spurning Saul's armour, the youth equipped only with his
staff and 'five smooth stones out of the brook', takes on Goliath. After
taunting each other, they engage in combat, David confident of God's
protection. 'Putting his hand in his bag, he took thence a stone and slang
it and smote the Philistine in the forehead that the stone sank into his
forehead and he fell upon his face to the earth. So David prevailed over
the Philistine with a sling and with a stone, and smote the Philistine and
slew him, but there was no sword in the hand of David' (1 Samuel
17.50). David became the champion of the weak over the strong and was
much celebrated for it. This great victory caused David to become the
darling of the women of Jerusalem. Saul's jealously grew and David
became a fugitive until he eventually succeeded to the throne. This boss
shows him enjoying his first victory which marked him as the icon of every
oppressed people. The city of Florence, constantly besieged by powerful
bullies, made David their champion, employing Donatello and
Michaelangelo to celebrate this same event in stone. The masons of
Norwich have fixed their less famous but endearing representation not on
a pedestal but suspended in the sky.

## 26. Solomon is crowned

At each coronation since the time of George II, Handel's famous anthem
has reminded us that 'Zadok the priest and Nathan the prophet anointed
Solomon King (1 Kings 1. 38–40) and all the people rejoiced'. These
words from the first book of Kings are the successful outcome of a long
and complicated dynastic struggle as to who would succeed to the throne
after David. The masons who carved this boss of a medieval monarch
sitting enthroned were no strangers to such dynastic wars. Solomon
represented a brief golden age when the Kingdom was untroubled, the
Temple completed and royal visitors like the Queen of Sheba (another of
Handel's subjects!) came to pay their respects and marvel at all that
Solomon had achieved. The Wars of the Roses made for a good parallel
for what preceded and followed Solomon's reign.

This glorious boss which completes our cycle, typifies much of what we
have seen in the stone vaults of Norwich Cathedral. Those who
commissioned this work were concerned to provide a secure and
permanent covering for this great house of God as evidenced in the
completion of the magnificent stone vault in which these bosses are set.
They wished to celebrate the history of salvation as it is revealed in Holy
Scripture, and to make connections between the Old and New
Testaments. Most of all, they wanted to tell a story that connected with
their daily lives. As the Lierne ribbed vaulting connects the fabric to the
roof, they were concerned to show how the whole of life was woven into a
rich tapestry of the sacred and secular. Clearly, medieval man was only
too happy to make links between the Bible and his own situation. Hence,
we see Solomon here looking like Edward IV sitting in state and holding,
not a model of the new Jerusalem Temple, but of Norwich Cathedral.
This boss celebrates the completion of a great work. Once the bosses
were finished, they represented the crowning glory of a great Cathedral.
Solomon looks down in splendour from a vantage point which overarches
a grand design. We salute the people who were inspired to carve these
stone bosses, which still have a message for those who will look up and
read this story for themselves.